NIST Technical Note 1800

Test Report - Exposure and Ambient Dose Equivalent Rate Measurements in Support of the ITRAP+10 Testing

L. Pibida
R. Minniti
M. O'Brien
L. Lucas

Radiation and Biomolecular Physics Division
Physical Measurement Laboratory

May 2013

U.S. Department of Commerce
Rebecca Blank, Acting Secretary

National Institute of Standards and Technology
Patrick D. Gallagher, Under Secretary of Commerce for Standards and Technology and Director

Test Report - Exposure and Ambient Dose Equivalent Rate Measurements in Support of the ITRAP+10 Testing

L. Pibida, R. Minniti, M. O'Brien, and L. Lucas

National Institute of Standards and Technology, 100 Bureau Dr, Gaithersburg, MD 20899-8462

Abstract

In this work we studied the response of two different Victoreen® instruments as a function of the exposure rate, the instrument orientation and photon energy. The rate dependence for both instruments is of the order of 8 % over the range of exposure rates tested (0.5 mR/h to 1000 mR/h). Regarding the instrument orientation dependence investigation, a significant difference is observed between the two instruments. While the Victoreen® 451P shows no significant dependence with instrument orientation, the Victoreen® 451P-DE-SI shows a significant dependence of up to 20 % between the three different orientations. Finally, the energy dependence measurements of both instruments reveal that the instruments measure lower exposure rate values compared to the reference values for the low energy x-rays by about 20 %. While, for the ^{60}Co gamma-ray beam measurements, both instruments are about 5 % higher than the reference value.

Key words:

exposure rate, ambient dose equivalent rate, ITRAP+10 testing, Victoreen 451P, Victoreen 451P-DE-SI

Introduction

The US Department of Homeland Security (DHS) Domestic Nuclear Detection Office (DNDO) requested the National Institute of Standards and Technology (NIST) to perform a set of measurements to validate exposure rate and ambient dose equivalent rate measurements performed during the Illicit Trafficking Radiation Assessment Program (ITRAP+10) testing program.

The ITRAP+10 is a program initiated by the European Union (EU) that carried out an evaluation of commercial available radiation detection equipment against published consensus standards. The standards used for testing included those published by the American National Standard Institute/ Institute of Electrical and Electronics Engineers (ANSI/IEEE) and the International Electrotechnical Commission (IEC). The European Commission's (EC) Joint Research Center (JRC), and DNDO agreed to collaborate in conducting the ITRAP+10 test campaign and sharing the design of the tests, their execution, the data, and the analysis of the data. Testing was carried out at the JRC and several DOE National Laboratories. There were nine different categories of instruments tested under the ITRAP+10 program, these included:

- Personal Radiation Detectors (PRDs)
- Spectroscopic Personal Radiation Detectors (SPRDs)

- Backpack-type Radiation Detectors (BRDs)
- Radiation Isotope Identification Device (RIIDs)
- Radiation Portal Monitor (RPMs)
- Spectroscopic Radiation Portal Monitor (SRPMs)
- Mobile Systems
- Neutron Search Devices (NSDs)
- Gamma Search Devices (GSDs)

Testing of the PRDs took place at the JRC and at the Savannah River National Laboratory (SRNL). Several tests defined in the ITRAP+10 test methods, based on the ANSI/IEEE and IEC standards, require determining the ambient dose equivalent rate produced by ^{241}Am (or x-rays), ^{137}Cs and ^{60}Co sources. For determining the radiation fields, the JRC used a Victoreen® 451P-DE-SI[1] pressurized ionization chamber and SRNL used a Victoreen® 451P. The Victoreen® 451P is a pressurized ionization chamber instrument calibrated in exposure rate units of roentgens/hour [2] for gamma-ray and x-ray radiation in the energy range of 20 keV to 2 MeV with a case built of high strength plastic. The Victoreen® 451P-DE-SI is a similar pressurized ionization chamber instrument calibrated in terms of the ambient dose equivalent rate ($\dot{H}^*(10)$) in units of sieverts/hour for the same energy range of gamma-ray and x-ray radiation. The energy and angular response of these two Victoreen® models is different, see instrument manual [1]. The Victoreen® 451P used at SRNL was calibrated in a ^{137}Cs beam and the Victoreen® 451P-DE-SI used at the JRC was calibrated in an x-ray (L2 beam quality), ^{137}Cs and ^{60}Co beams.

Due to differences observed in the PRD test results during the ITRAP+10, DNDO requested NIST to perform several measurements using a Victoreen® 451P-DE-SI and a Victoreen® 451P to assess the differences in the instrument radiation response as a function the exposure rate, instrument orientation and gamma-ray and x-ray energy. The results of these measurements are summarized here.

Test facilities and experimental setup

Four different NIST primary measurement facilities, see Figure 1, were used to perform the proposed measurements; two deliver low and high intensity ^{137}Cs gamma-ray reference beams while the other two facilities deliver ^{60}Co gamma-ray and x-ray beams [3, 4].

The NIST primary reference beams provide a well-defined value of air-kerma rate (in units of Gy/s) and exposure rate (in units of R/s) at a given point in space. The uncertainties of the exposure rate values delivered by these reference beams are well

---

[1] Mention of commercial products does not imply recommendation nor endorsement by the National Institute of Standards and Technology, nor does it imply that the products identified are necessarily the best available for the purpose.

[2] NIST does not endorse the use of non-SI units. This paper uses non-SI units because it addresses the requirements listed in the TCS published standards and the units displayed by the test equipment.

known and have values of less than 0.5 %. The following exposure rates can be obtained in the different measurement facilities:

- ^{137}Cs lower intensity reference beams

    - 500 μR/h to 1 mR/h

    - 5 mR/h to 15 mR/h

    - 90 mR/h to 300 mR/h

- ^{137}Cs higher intensity reference beam – 500 mR/h to 10 R/h

- ^{60}Co reference beam – 52 mR/h to 120 mR/h

- x-ray reference beam depends on the beam quality

    - NS80 (corresponds to the N80 ISO 4037 beam with a mean energy of 65 keV) – greater than 127 mR/h

    - WS80 (corresponds to the L2 beam used by the JRC and the W80 ISO 4037 beam with a mean energy of 57 keV) – greater than 370 mR/h

Additional measurements using an ^{241}Am source, with a gamma-ray emission rate of 4.11 $\times 10^7$ gammas/s (± 5%), were performed by placing the source at a distance of 1 m from the reference point of the Victoreen® 451P and the Victoreen® 451P-DE-SI respectively. As there is no air-kerma or exposure rate primary standard in the U.S. for ^{241}Am, there is no reference exposure rate value available for these measurements. These measurements can be used to obtain the relative response of the Victoreen® 451P and the Victoreen® 451P-DE-SI in the three measurement orientations (front, right side, and left side).

The reference point marked on the instrument was aligned at the point in space where the air-kerma rate value is defined. The Victoreen® 451P was placed free in air at the point in space where the exposure rate field has the required value, see Figure 2. The Victoreen® 451P was mounted on an aluminum stand in order to reduce scattering. An aligning laser system was used to position the Victoreen® 451P.

The Victoreen® 451P was placed in the reference beam in three different orientations with the front, right and left side of the instrument facing the source as shown in Figure 2. For each orientation of the instrument, three independent sets of data were recorded. Each set was composed of 30 exposure rate readings. In order to obtain the three independent measurement sets, the Victoreen® 451P was removed and placed back at the measurement point three times. For each set, the recording of the exposure rate readings was started 30 s after the source shutter was opened (source exposed). This 30 s delay time between the time the shutter is opened and the recording of data was to allow the Victoreen® 451P instruments to reach a stable value (settling time). These measurements were repeated for the Victoreen® 451P-DE-SI (serial number 3500). For some of the measurements two different Victoreen® 451P units were used (serial number 3796 and 2396) in order to check for reproducibility in the instrument response.

The maximum exposure rate that the Victoreen® 451P can measure is 5 R/h and the maximum ambient dose equivalent rate that the Victoreen® 451P-DE-SI can measure is 50 mSv/h [1], so the exposure rates selected for the measurements were kept below 5 R/h. The cut-off energy of the instruments is 25 keV.

In order to cover several of the instrument exposure rate ranges, NIST performed the measurements at the following exposure and air-kerma rate values:

- ^{137}Cs – 500 µR/h (4.390 µGy/h), 15 mR/h (131.7 µGy/h), 100 mR/h (0.878 mGy/h), 500.3 mR/h (4.391 mGy/h), and 1 R/h (8.784 mGy/h)

- ^{60}Co – 100.3 mR/h (0.822 mGy/h)

- x-ray beam NS80 – 142.9 mR/h (1.253 mGy/h) at 3 m, 129.1 mR/h (1.118 mGy/h) at 2 m, and 517.8 mR/h (4.538 mGy/h) at 2 m

- x-ray beam WS80 –approximately 482.4 mR/h (4.248 mGy/h) at 3 m

The mean energy for the NS80 and the WS80 x-ray beams are 65 keV and 57 keV respectively.

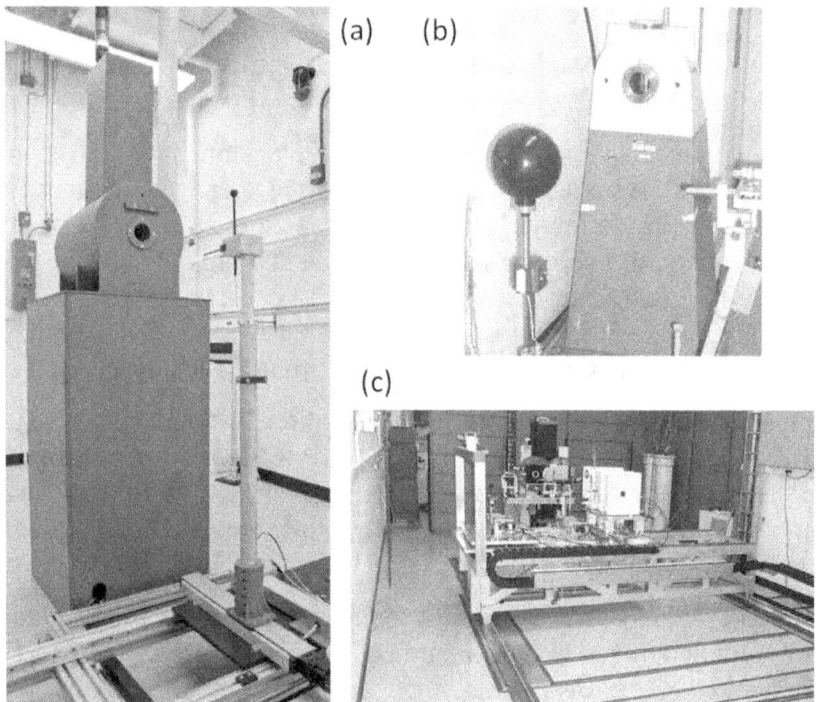

Figure 1: NIST reference beams: (a) ^{137}Cs, (b) ^{60}Co, (c) x-ray measurement facilities

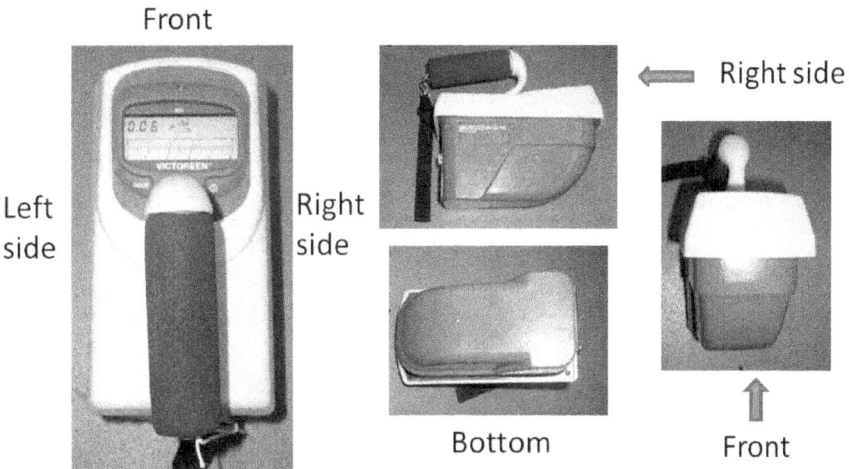

Figure 2: Shown are the reference points of the Victoreen® 451P and orientations

Data analysis

The average and standard deviation for the 30 readings for each measurement set was calculated. The three independent measurements were combined to obtain the Victoreen® 451P instrument average response for each orientation and beam and/or beam code. The Victoreen® 451P instrument response was compared to the actual value of the exposure rate delivered by the reference field, then the percent difference to the reference value was calculated for each beam and Victoreen® 451P orientation (front, right side and left side). This procedure was repeated for the Victoreen® 451P-DE-SI.

The following conversion coefficients obtained from [3] were applied to the Victoreen® 451P-DE-SI readings in order to convert ambient dose equivalent rate to air-kerma rate and exposure rate to air-kerma:

- For ^{137}Cs – 1.20 Sv/Gy and 113.92 R/Gy
- For ^{60}Co – 1.16 Sv/Gy and 113.74 R/Gy
- For ^{241}Am – 1.74 Sv/Gy and 114.10 R/Gy
- For NS80 (N80 ISO 4037) x-ray beam – 1.73 Sv/Gy and 114.10 R/Gy
- For WS80 (W80 ISO 4037) x-ray beam – 1.66 Sv/Gy and 114.10 R/Gy

For the ^{241}Am measurements of the exposure rate and ambient dose equivalent rate values were plotted as a function of the instrument orientation. The ambient dose equivalent rate values of the Victoreen® 451P-DE-SI were converted to exposure rate for the comparison of instrument response. The exposure rate produced by the ^{241}Am could be calculated using exposure rate constants. The problem with this approach is the large discrepancies found among the published constants [5, 7, 9, 11, 12 and 13]. The exposure rate constant calculated using different methods at 1 m are listed in Table 1. The calculations in references [11 and 12] use a cut-off energy of 1 keV, the same value used in the Monte Carlo calculation performed using MCNPX by references [7, 9 and 10]. The difference

5

between the two MCNPX (LNHB) and MCNPX (NBL) exposure rate constant calculations are the values used for the gamma-ray emission probabilities for the different ^{241}Am photon energies. The first one makes use of the values listed in reference [10] and the other in reference [9].

Table 1: List of calculated exposure rate constants

Exposure rate constant (R m^2/h/Ci)							
Point source estimate cut-off energy 1 keV [5, 9]	Point source estimate cut-off energy 25 keV [5, 9]	Point source estimate cut-off energy 40 keV [5, 9]	MCNPX (LNHB) [7, 10]	MCNPX (NBL) [7, 9]	Smith et al. [11]	Seltzer [13]	Rad Pro calculator [12]
0.0925	0.01797	0.0155	0.1189	0.097	0.0749	0.0962	0.0166

The calculated exposure rate for the ^{241}Am source using the different exposure rate constant values listed in Table 1 at 1 m are shown in Table 2. Based on this large variation observed between the different calculated values it is not possible to compare the instruments measured with a reference exposure rate value.

Table 2: Calculate exposure rates for the ^{241}Am source at a 1 m distance

Exposure rate at 1 m (R/h)							
Point source estimate cut-off energy 1 keV [5, 9]	Point source estimate cut-off energy 25 keV [5, 9]	Point source estimate cut-off energy 40 keV [5, 9]	MCNPX (LNHB) [7, 10]	MCNPX (NBL) [7, 9]	Smith et al. [11]	Seltzer [13]	Rad Pro calculator [12]
287	55.8	48.1	369	301	233	299	51.6

It is important to note that when setting an ambient dose equivalent rate field (Sv/h) with an instrument that measures exposure rate (R/h) the right conversion coefficient shall be used in the field determination. The same is true when trying to set up an exposure rate field (R/h) with an instrument that measures ambient dose equivalent rate (Sv/h).

The percent difference between the instrument mean reading and the NIST reference exposure rate value was calculated for each beam quality and instrument orientation. A calibration factor for the 500 mR/h ^{137}Cs beam for each instrument orientation was determined as the ratio between the NIST reference exposure rate value and the instrument mean reading. The calibration factor can be applied to the instrument readings for the other beam qualities in order to normalize the reading to a reference value.

Measurement results

The Victoreen® 451P and the Victoreen® 451P-DE-SI readings were monitored beginning at the start of the exposure in order to establish the time at which the readings became stable. For all beams it took approximately 5 seconds to reach a stable reading.

The x-ray beam measurements were repeated on two different days and the results for both instruments, the Victoreen® 451P and the Victoreen® 451P-DE-SI, are summarized in Table 3. For the Victoreen® 451P two different units were used on each day. The ^{137}Cs measurements are summarized in Table 4. The ^{60}Co measurements are summarized in Table 5. As described previously, each exposure rate shown in the Table corresponds to the average of three sets of measurements, where each set was composed of a total of 30 readings.

The Victoreen® 451P and the Victoreen® 451P-DE-SI are normally used as survey meters for health physics applications. These types of instruments are only required to be calibrated in a ^{137}Cs reference field at different exposure rates. In this work we calibrated the Victoreen® 451P and the Victoreen® 451P-DE-SI instruments in the x-ray (NS80 and WS80 beam qualities) ^{137}Cs and ^{60}Co reference beams. The measured calibration factors obtained in each one of these reference fields are listed in Table 6, Table 7 and

Table 8 for the ^{137}Cs and ^{60}Co reference beams and in Table 9, Table 10 and Table 11 for the x-ray reference beams.

The paragraphs below summarize the results obtained from studying the response of these instruments as a function of exposure rate, instrument orientation and beam energy. The measured exposure rate dependence is shown in Figures 3 and 4 for the ^{137}Cs beam and Figures 5 and 7 for the x-ray beam. The exposure rate dependence for each radiation beam (^{137}Cs and NS80 x-rays) is also presented for each of the three possible instrument orientations: front, right and left. For the measurements presented in Figures 3 and 4, the calibration factor used for both Victoreen instruments was the one obtained at an exposure rate of 500 mR/h in the ^{137}Cs reference beam. From these figures it can be observed that there is approximately an 8 % variation in the response of both the Victoreen® 451P and Victoreen® 451P-DE-SI for exposure rates between 500 μR/h and 1 R/h for ^{137}Cs. For the x-ray measurement results presented in Figure 5 and Figure 6, the calibration factor used for both Victoreen instruments was the one obtained in the NS80 x-ray reference beam at a distance of 2 m using the exposure rate value of approximately 500 mR/h. This data point is referred to in Figures 5 and 6 as the 2 m High Rate setting. From these figures it can be observed that there is approximately a 5 % variation in the response of both the Victoreen® 451P (for both serial numbers) and Victoreen® 451P-DE-SI for exposure rates between 100 mR/h and 500 mR/h for the 2 m and 3 m measurement distances for the NS80 beam code. The WS80 beam code was performed at a single rate of 500 mR/h at a distance of 3 m; from these figures a difference of approximately 7 % can be observed between the NS80 and WS80 beam qualities for the Victoreen® 451P (for both serial numbers). For the Victoreen® 451P-DE-SI the difference in response between the NS80 and WS80 beam codes varies between -10 % and 2 % depending on the instrument orientation.

The dependence of the instrument response as a function of the instrument orientation (front, right and left) was also investigated. The results are summarized in Figures 7 and 8 for the Victoreen 451P and 451P-DE-SI detectors respectively. The orientation dependence was obtained in the NS80 and WS80 x-ray, ^{137}Cs and ^{60}Co reference beams. The calibration factor for each of the instruments used for the measurement results presented in Figures 7 and 8 was the one obtained in the ^{137}Cs reference beam at the measured exposure rates of 100 mR/h and 500 mR/h. The ^{137}Cs calibration factor of 100 mR/h was used for the measurements made in the NS80 x-ray, ^{137}Cs, and ^{60}Co beams that delivered rates of 100 mR/h (shown as solid symbols in Figures 7 and 8) on the instruments. The ^{137}Cs calibration factor of 500 mR/h was used for the measurements made in the ^{137}Cs, WS80 and NS80 x-ray beams that delivered exposure rates of 500 mR/h (shown as hollow symbols in Figures 7 and 8). The data point for the NS80 x-ray shown in Figures 7 and 8 corresponds to the average of the instrument readings over all measured distances (2 m and 3 m). Figure 7 indicates that there is a small dependence with the instrument orientation for the case of the Victoreen® 451P. The variation observed between all three orientations is within 1 %. However the dependence of the instrument orientation for the variation observed for the Victoreen® 451P-DE-SI is quite significant and it is dependent on the beam quality or beam energy. For example, Figure

8 shows clearly that the readings obtained using the Front orientation are about 20% lower than those obtained when the detector faces the source sideways (Right or Left orientation). Similarly, the measurements made in the NS80 beam also show a strong orientation dependence. The detector readings obtained with the front of the detector facing the source are 15 % lower in value than those obtained with the detector facing sideways (Right or Left orientations).

The energy dependence for the Victoreen® 451P (serial number 2396) and the Victoreen® 451P-DE-SI detectors at two different exposure rates of 100 mR/h and 500 mR/h are shown in Figure 9. At each exposure rate and orientation the calibration factor used was obtained for the ^{137}Cs reference beam. The x-ray beam measurements average over all measured distances. From this figure it can be observed that for the Victoreen® 451P-DE-SI the response drops with energy, and a larger variation is observed when measurements are performed from the front. For the Victoreen® 451P there is a similar energy variation but the differences between the front and the sides are smaller.

In order to assess the possible differences in the Victoreen® 451P or Victoreen® 451P-DE-SI response due to instrument volume, x-ray measurements were performed at the high exposure rate value at 1 m and 2 m from the source, see Figure 10. From this figure it can be observed that, as expected, the response from the side at 1 m is much lower (6 % to 8 %) than the response measured from the front (2 %). This is due to the large volume presented by the instrument when measuring from the side.

The ^{241}Am measurements are summarized in Figure 11. After applying the conversion coefficient (from Sv to R) to the Victoreen® 451P-DE-SI ambient dose equivalent rate readings it can be observed that there is no difference in response for the Victoreen® 451P or Victoreen® 451P-DE-SI within the measured uncertainty. Still the difference in response for the Victoreen® 451P-DE-SI between the front and side orientations is larger than for the Victoreen® 451P.

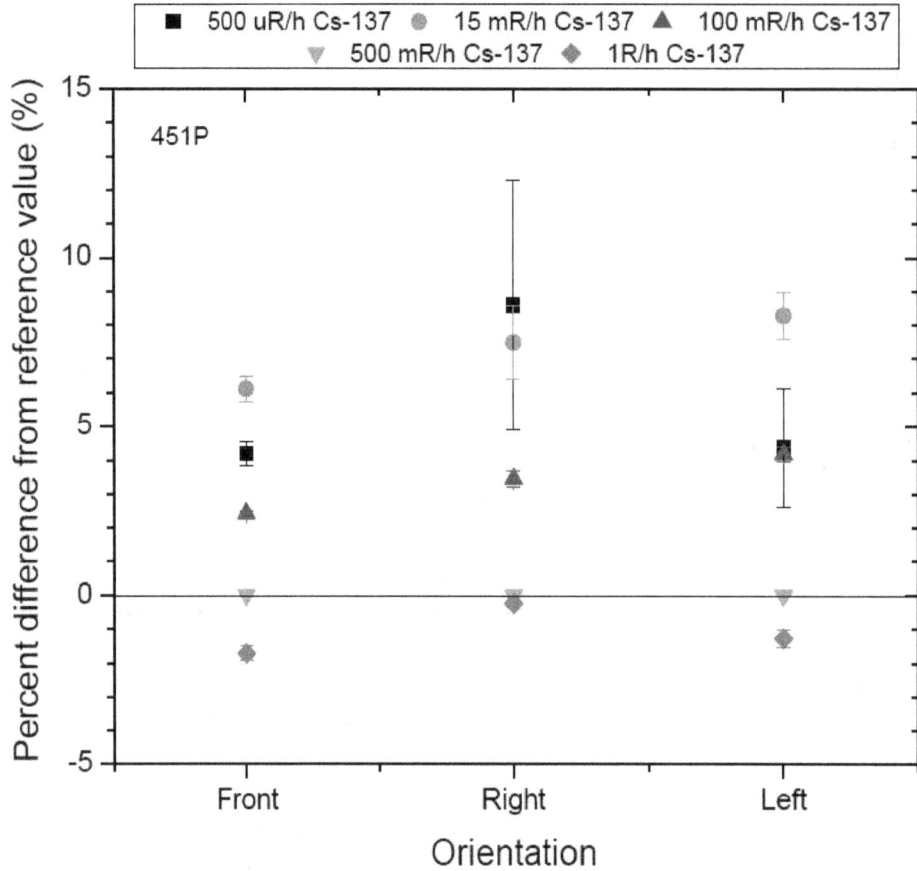

Figure 3: Rate dependence for the 451P (serial number 2396) detector for the ^{137}Cs reference beams. At each exposure rate and orientation the calibration factor used was obtained at the 500 mR/h for the ^{137}Cs reference beam. Uncertainties are one standard deviation.

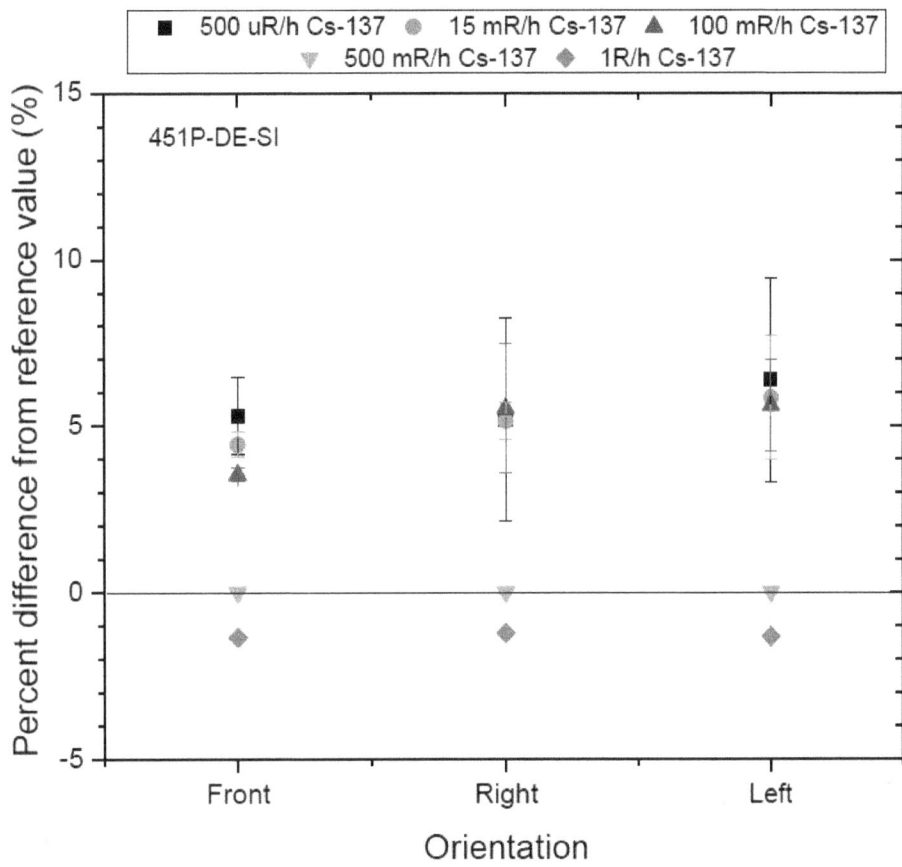

Figure 4: Rate dependence for the 451P-DE-SI detector for the ^{137}Cs reference beams. At each exposure rate and orientation the calibration factor used was obtained at the 500 mR/h for the ^{137}Cs reference beam. Uncertainties are one standard deviation.

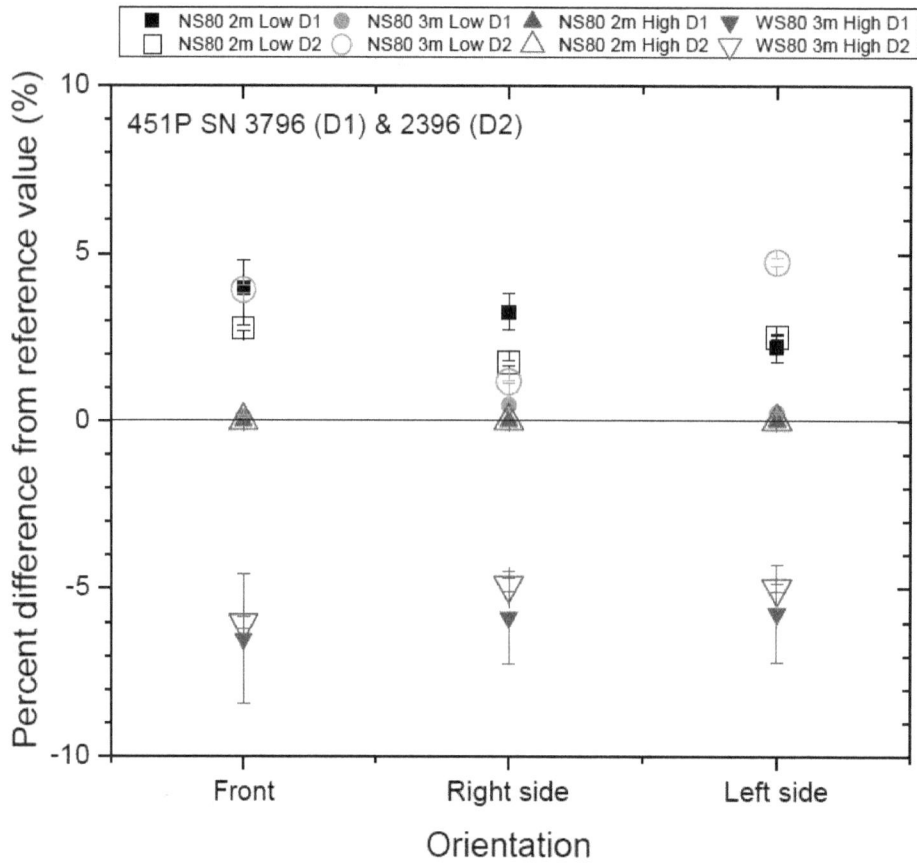

Figure 5: Rate dependence for the 451P detector for the x-ray reference beams. At each exposure rate and orientation the calibration factor used was obtained at the 2 m High (500 mR/h) for the x-ray reference beam. The solid symbols represent the unit with serial number 3796 and the open symbols for the serial number 2396. Uncertainties are one standard deviation.

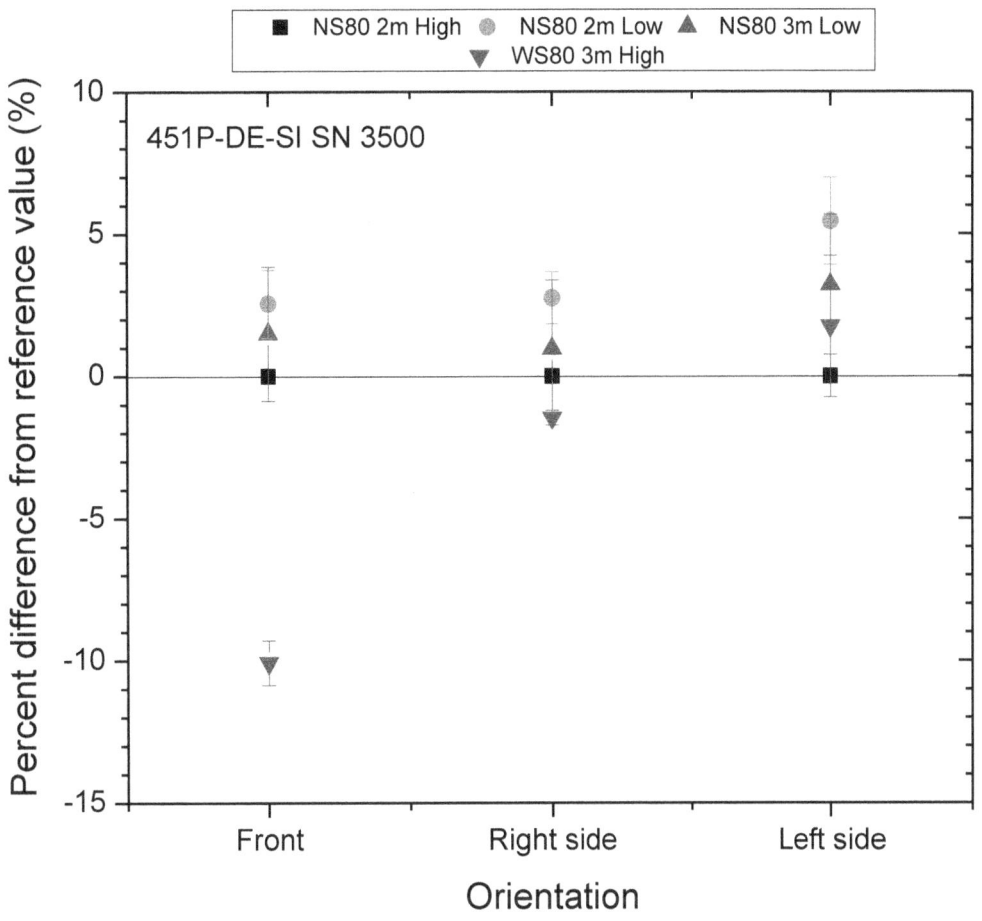

Figure 6: Rate dependence for the 451P-DE-SI detector for the x-ray reference beams. At each exposure rate and orientation the calibration factor used was obtained at the 2 m High (482.4 mR/h) for the x-ray reference beam. The values are the average between the two day measurements. Uncertainties are one standard deviation.

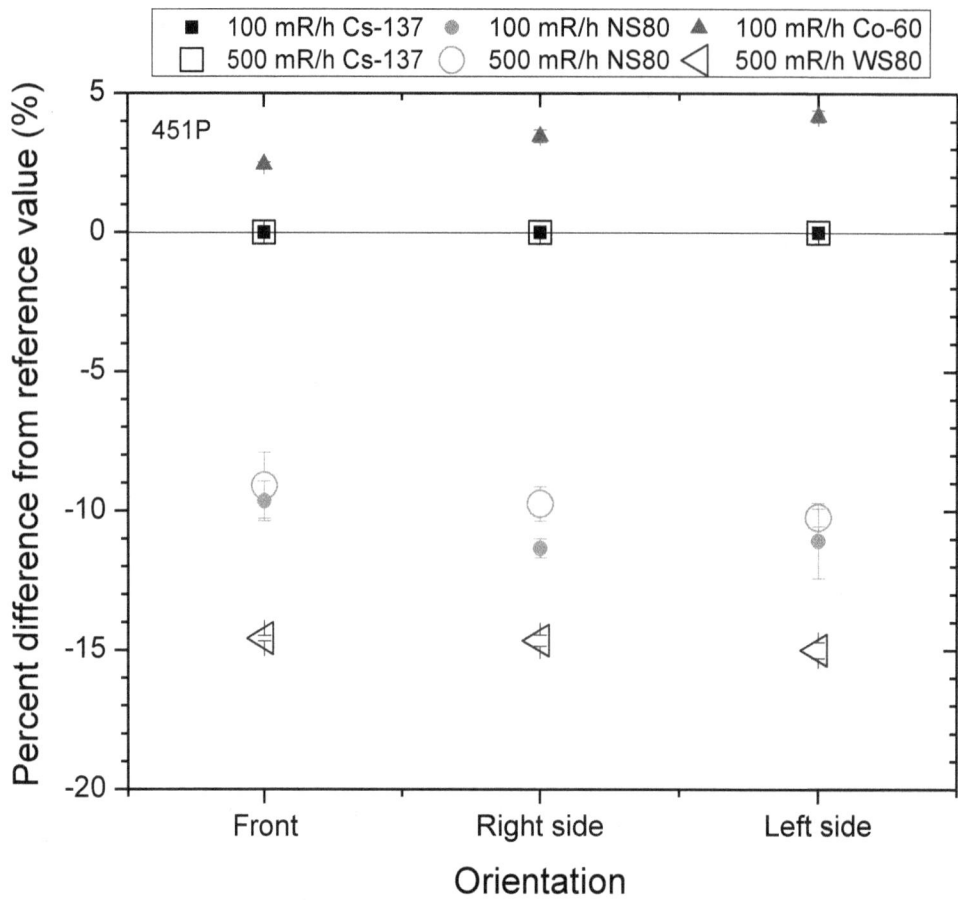

Figure 7: Orientation dependence for the 451P (serial number 2396) detector at two different exposure rates of approximately 100 mR/h and 500 mR/h. At each exposure rate and orientation the calibration factor used was obtained for the ^{137}Cs reference beam. The x-ray beam measurements average over all measured distance. Uncertainties are one standard deviation.

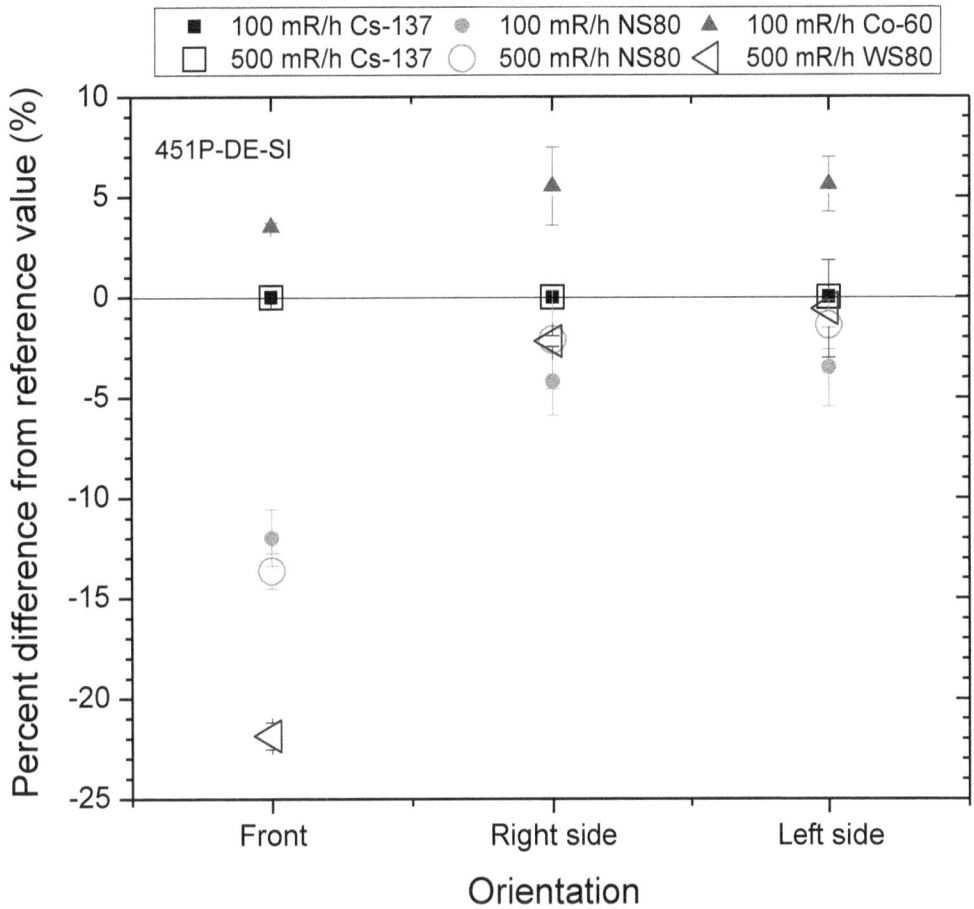

Figure 8: Orientation dependence for the 451P-DE-SI detector at two different exposure rates of approximately 100 mR/h and 500 mR/h. At each exposure rate and orientation the calibration factor used was obtained for the ^{137}Cs reference beam. The x-ray beam measurements averaged over all measured distances. Uncertainties are one standard deviation.

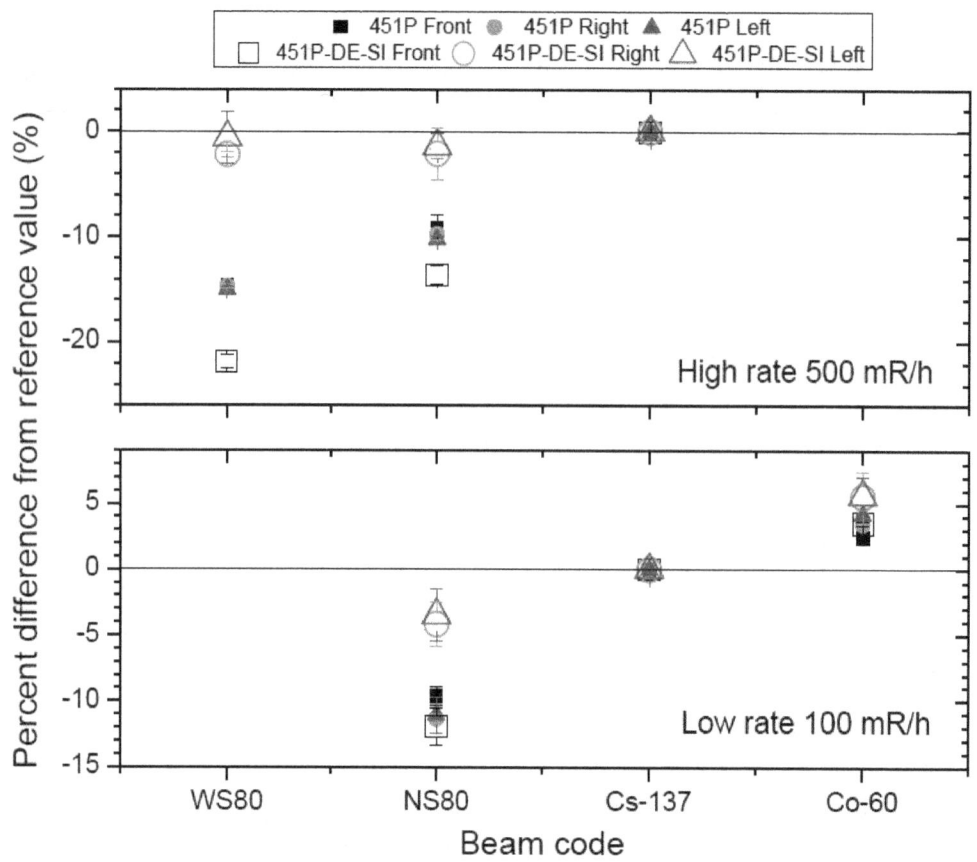

Figure 9: Beam energy dependence for the 451P (serial number 2396) and the 451P-DE-SI detectors at two different exposure rates of approximately 100 mR/h and 500 mR/h. At each exposure rate and orientation the calibration factor used was obtained for the ^{137}Cs reference beam. The x-ray beam measurements averaged over all measured distances. Uncertainties are one standard deviation.

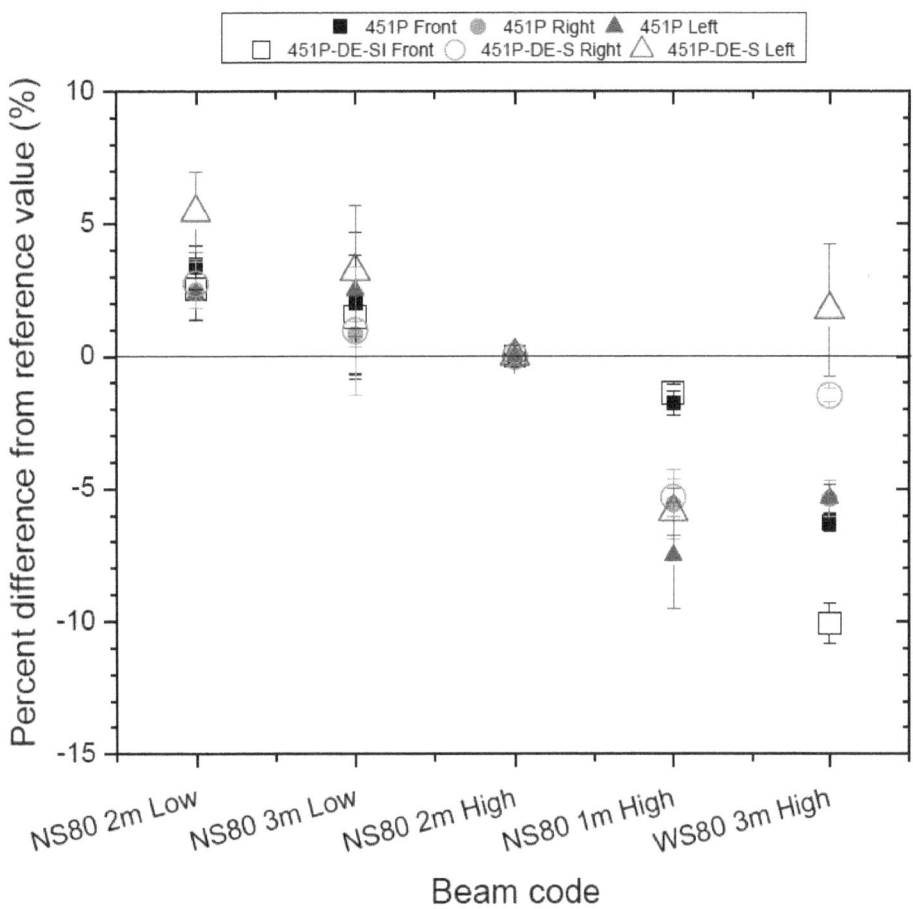

Figure 10: Comparison of the measured percent difference from reference value for the 451P and 451P-DE-SI instruments with measurements obtained using a NIST ionization chamber. At each exposure rate and orientation the calibration factor used was obtained at the 2 m High (482.4 mR/h) for the x-ray reference beam. Uncertainties are one standard deviation.

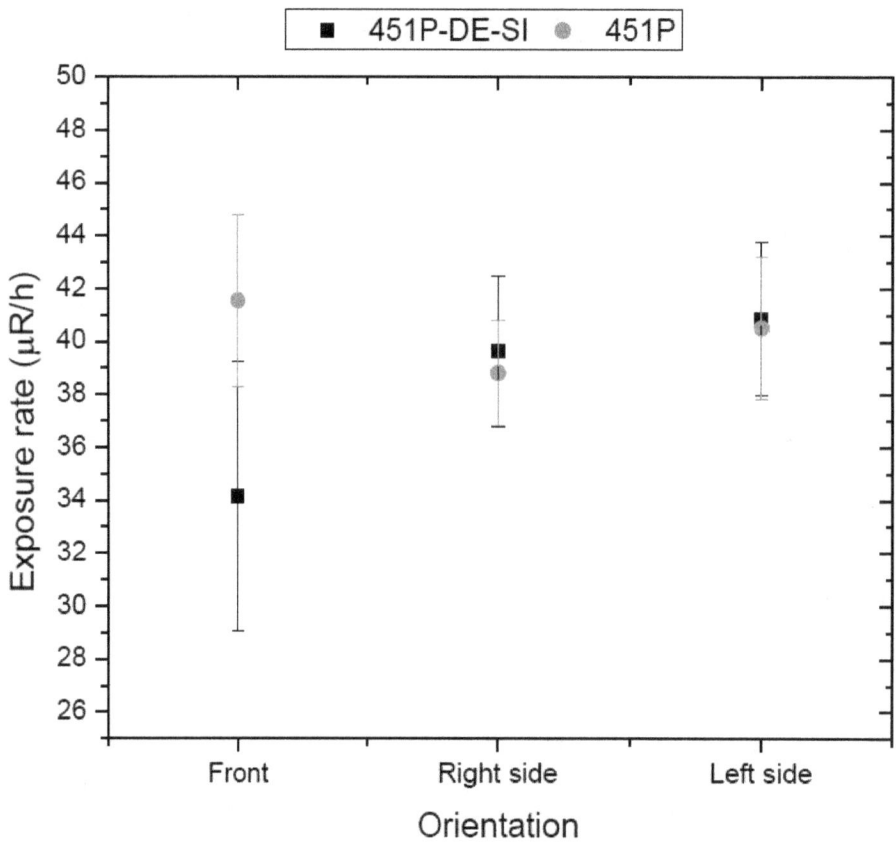

Figure 11: Measured exposure rate value for the 451P and 451P-DE-SI instruments as a function of the instrument orientation for [241]Am source. The red circles represent the results for the 451P and the black squares represent the results for the 451P-DE-SI instrument. Uncertainties are one standard deviation.

Table 3: Summary of the 451P and 451P-DE-SI instrument background subtracted readings for the different x-ray beam configurations without applying the conversion coefficient (Sv/Gy) and the ^{137}Cs calibration factor

X-ray beam configuration	Reference beam exposure and air-kerma rates	Victoreen® 451P		Victoreen® 451P-DE-SI	
		Average exposure rate readings (mR/h)	Standard deviation (%)	Average ambient dose rate readings (mSv/h)	Standard deviation (%)
Front - First day Victoreen® 451P SN: 3796					
NS80 2 m Low	127.6 mR/h or 1.118 mGy/h (± 0.57 %)	99.98	0.05	1.56	0.07
NS80 3 m Low	142.9 mR/h or 1.253 mGy/h (± 0.37 %)	107.88	0.08	1.69	0.02
NS80 2 m High	517.8 mR/h or 4.538 mGy/h (± 0.45 %)	390.33	0.00	6.12	0.41
WS80 3 m High	482.4 mR/h or 4.248 mGy/h (± 0.5 %)	339.99	0.00	4.91	1.24
Right side- First day Victoreen® 451P SN: 3796					
NS80 2 m Low	127.6 µR/h or 1.118 mGy/h (± 0.57 %)	108.59	0.12	1.86	0.16
NS80 3 m Low	142.9 µR/h or 1.253 mGy/h (± 0.37 %)	117.02	0.40	2.00	0.04
NS80 2 m High	517.8 mR/h or 4.538 mGy/h (± 0.45 %)	421.88	0.33	7.30	0.18
WS80 3 m High	482.4 mR/h or 4.248 mGy/h (± 0.5 %)	370.00	0.00	6.44	0.71
Left side - First day Victoreen® 451P SN: 3796					
NS80 2 m Low	127.6 µR/h or 1.118 mGy/h (± 0.57 %)	104.41	0.24	1.87	0.22
NS80 3 m Low	142.9 µR/h or 1.253 mGy/h (± 0.37 %)	113.42	0.16	2.00	0.06
NS80 2 m High	517.8 mR/h or 4.538 mGy/h (± 0.45 %)	409.87	0.09	7.14	1.20
WS80 3 m High	482.4 mR/h or 4.248 mGy/h (± 0.5 %)	359.99	0.00	6.41	1.54
Front - Second day Victoreen® 451P SN: 2396					

X-ray beam configuration	Reference beam exposure and air-kerma rates	Victoreen® 451P		Victoreen® 451P-DE-SI	
		Average exposure rate readings (mR/h)	Standard deviation (%)	Average ambient dose rate readings (mSv/h)	Standard deviation (%)
NS80 2 m Low	129.8 mR/h or 1.138 mGy/h (± 1.13 %)	100.13	0.73	1.56	0.58
NS80 3 m Low	138.2 mR/h or 1.211 mGy/h (± 0.76 %)	107.79	0.82	1.69	0.67
NS80 2 m High	519.6 mR/h or 4.553 mGy/h (± 0.15 %)	390.00	0.00	6.14	0.81
WS80 3 m High	482.0 mR/h or 4.225 mGy/h (± 0.16 %)	340.00	0.00	4.95	1.38
Right side - Second day Victoreen® 451P SN: 2396					
NS80 2 m Low	129.8 mR/h or 1.138 mGy/h (± 1.13 %)	106.60	0.84	1.87	0.47
NS80 3 m Low	138.2 mR/h or 1.211 mGy/h (± 0.76 %)	112.86	0.86	2.00	0.15
NS80 2 m High	519.6 mR/h or 4.553 mGy/h (± 0.15 %)	419.33	0.61	6.99	0.62
WS80 3 m High	482.0 mR/h or 4.225 mGy/h (± 0.16 %)	370.00	0.00	6.43	0.75
Left side - Second day Victoreen® 451P SN: 2396					
NS80 2 m Low	129.8 mR/h or 1.138 mGy/h (± 1.13 %)	104.66	0.81	1.87	1.03
NS80 3 m Low	138.2 mR/h or 1.211 mGy/h (± 0.76 %)	113.86	0.79	2.00	0.09
NS80 2 m High	519.6 mR/h or 4.553 mGy/h (± 0.15 %)	408.66	0.85	7.19	0.35
WS80 3 m High	482.0 mR/h or 4.225 mGy/h (± 0.16 %)	360.30	0.46	6.60	0.00

Table 4: Summary of the 451P and 451P-DE-SI instrument background subtracted readings for the different ^{137}Cs beam configurations without applying the conversion coefficient ((Sv/Gy) and the ^{137}Cs calibration factor

^{137}Cs beam configuration	Reference beam exposure and air-kerma rates	Victoreen® 451P		Victoreen® 451P-DE-SI	
		Average exposure rate readings (mR/h)	Standard deviation (%)	Average ambient dose rate readings (mSv/h)	Standard deviation (%)
		Front - Victoreen® 451P SN: 2396			
500 µR/h (230.2 cm)	500 µR/h or 4.390 µGy/h (± 0.5 %)	0.43676	1.09	0.00484	1.91
15 mR/h (210.1 cm)	15 mR/h or 131.7 µGy/h (± 0.5 %)	13.34	0.66	0.14408	0.80
100 mR/h (344.1 cm)	100 mR/h or 0.878 mGy/h (± 0.5 %)	85.86	0.19	0.95	0.53
500 mR/h (275.2 m)	500.26 mR/h or 4.391 mGy/h (± 0.5 %)	419.32	0.28	4.60	0.00
1 R/h (195.2 cm)	1.00 R/h or 8.784 mGy/h (± 0.5 %)	824	2.52	9.08	0.70
		Right side- Victoreen® 451P SN: 2396			
500 µR/h (230.2 cm)	500 µR/h or 4.390 µGy/h (± 0.5 %)	0.4848	0.95	0.00522	0.48
15 mR/h (210.1 cm)	15 mR/h or 131.7 µGy/h (± 0.5 %)	14.40	0.58	0.15659	0.59
100 mR/h (344.1 cm)	100 mR/h or 0.878 mGy/h (± 0.5 %)	92.37	0.40	1.04	0.43
500 mR/h (275.2 m)	500.26 mR/h or 4.391 mGy/h (± 0.5 %)	446.66	0.34	4.93	0.85
1 R/h (195.2 cm)	1.00 R/h or 8.784 mGy/h (± 0.5 %)	891	0.19	9.75	0.37
		Left side - Victoreen® 451P SN: 2396			
500 µR/h (230.2 cm)	500 µR/h or 4.390 µGy/h (± 0.5 %)	0.45911	3.02	0.00519	0.91
15 mR/h (210.1 cm)	15 mR/h or 131.7 µGy/h (± 0.5 %)	14.29	0.39	0.15466	0.22
100 mR/h (344.1 cm)	100 mR/h or 0.878 mGy/h (± 0.5 %)	91.65	0.40	1.04	0.42
500 mR/h	500.26 mR/h or	440.10	0.04	4.90	0.42

^{137}Cs beam configuration	Reference beam exposure and air-kerma rates	Victoreen® 451P		Victoreen® 451P-DE-SI	
		Average exposure rate readings (mR/h)	Standard deviation (%)	Average ambient dose rate readings (mSv/h)	Standard deviation (%)
(275.2 m)	4.391 mGy/h (± 0.5 %)				
1 R/h (195.2 cm)	1.00 R/h or 8.784 mGy/h (± 0.5 %)	869	3.07	9.68	0.33
		Front - Victoreen® 451P SN: 3796			
500 mR/h (275.2 m)	500.26 mR/h or 4.391 mGy/h (± 0.5 %)	412.44	0.96	NA	NA
		Right side - Victoreen® 451P SN: 3796			
500 mR/h (275.2 m)	500.26 mR/h or 4.391 mGy/h (± 0.5 %)	448.88	0.43	NA	NA
		Left side - Victoreen® 451P SN: 3796			
500 mR/h (275.2 m)	500.26 mR/h or 4.391 mGy/h (± 0.5 %)	440.22	0.09	NA	NA

Table 5: Summary of the 451P and 451P-DE-SI instrument background subtracted readings for the different ^{60}Co beam configurations without applying the conversion coefficient (Sv/Gy) and the ^{137}Cs calibration factor

^{60}Co beam configuration	Reference beam exposure and air-kerma rates	Victoreen® 451P		Victoreen® 451P-DE-SI	
		Average exposure rate readings (mR/h)	Standard deviation (%)	Average ambient dose rate readings (mSv/h)	Standard deviation (%)
		Front - Victoreen® 451P SN: 2396			
100 mR/h (215 cm)	100.29 mR/h or 0.882 mGy/h (± 0.5 %)	86.39	0.07	0.97	0.24
		Right side - Victoreen® 451P SN: 2396			
100 mR/h (215 cm)	100.29 mR/h or 0.882 mGy/h (± 0.5 %)	94.23	0.19	1.05	0.10
		Left side - Victoreen® 451P SN: 2396			
100 mR/h (215 cm)	100.29 mR/h or 0.882 mGy/h (± 0.5 %)	93.39	0.04	1.05	0.15

Table 6: Calibration factors determined in the ^{137}Cs and ^{60}Co reference beams for the Victoreen® 451P SN: 2396. The standard deviation of the measurement is shown below each value of the calibration factor. The additional underlined digits for the calibration factors are kept to avoid rounding errors when the values are used in the calculations, they do not represent the accuracy of the measured calibration factors.

451P, SN 2396		Co-60 100.00 mR/h	Cs-137 0.50 mR/h	Cs-137 15.00 mR/h	Cs-137 100.00 mR/h	Cs-137 500.00 mR/h	Cs-137 1000.00 mR/h	Cs-137 Combined
FRONT	Average	1.1608	1.1369	1.1239	1.1647	1.1930	1.2143	1.1666
	Std. Dev.	0.00	0.01	0.01	0.01	0.01	0.03	0.04
LEFT	Average	1.0854	1.0753	1.0495	1.0911	1.1199	1.1520	1.0976
	Std. Dev.	0.00	0.03	0.01	0.01	0.01	0.04	0.04
RIGHT	Average	1.0642	1.0221	1.0417	1.0826	1.1367	1.1227	1.0812
	Std. Dev.	0.00	0.01	0.01	0.01	0.00	0.01	0.05
BOTTOM	Average	NA	NA	1.0640	NA	NA	NA	NA
	Std. Dev.			0.01				

Table 7: Calibration factors determined in the ^{137}Cs reference beams for the Victoreen® 451P SN: 3796. The standard deviation of the measurement is shown below each value of the calibration factor. The additional underlined digits for the calibration factors are kept to avoid rounding errors when the values are used in the calculations, they do not represent the accuracy of the measured calibration factors.

451P, SN 3796		Cs-137 500.00 mR/h
FRONT	Average	**1.21<u>30</u>**
	Std. Dev.	0.01
LEFT	Average	**1.13<u>64</u>**
	Std. Dev.	0.01
RIGHT	Average	**1.11<u>45</u>**
	Std. Dev.	0.01

Table 8: Calibration factors determined in the ^{137}Cs and ^{60}Co reference beams for the 451P –DE-SI SN: 3500. The standard deviation of the measurement is shown below each value of the calibration factor. The additional underlined digits for the calibration factors are kept to avoid rounding errors when the values are used in the calculations, they do not represent the accuracy of the measured calibration factors.

451-DE-SI, SN 3500		Co-60 0.80 mGy/h	Cs-137 4.39 uGy/h	Cs-137 131.70 uGy/h	Cs-137 0.80 mGy/h	Cs-137 4.39 mGy/h	Cs-137 8.78 mGy/h	Cs-137 Combined
FRONT	Average	1.0492	1.0880	1.0970	1.1065	1.1145	1.1613	1.1135
	Std. Dev.	0.00	0.02	0.01	0.01	0.03	0.01	0.03
LEFT	Average	0.9777	1.0101	1.0219	1.0174	1.0745	1.0889	1.0426
	Std. Dev.	0.00	0.01	0.01	0.01	0.04	0.01	0.04
RIGHT	Average	0.9744	1.0157	1.0092	1.0123	1.0683	1.0814	1.0374
	Std. Dev.	0.00	0.01	0.01	0.01	0.01	0.01	0.04
BOTTOM	Average	NA	NA	1.0300	NA	NA	NA	NA
	Std. Dev.			0.01				

Table 9: Calibration factors calculated from the x-ray measurements for the Victoreen® 451P SN: 2396. The additional underlined digits for the calibration factors are kept to avoid rounding errors when the values are used in the calculations, they do not represent the accuracy of the measured calibration factors.

451P, SN 2396		NS80 (2 m Low) 129.81 mR/h	NS80 (3 m Low) 138.20 mR/h	NS80 (2 m High) 519.55 mR/h	WS80 (3 m High) 482.04 mR/h
FRONT	Average	1.2964	1.2820	1.3322	1.4178
	Std. Dev.	0.00	0.00	0.00	0.00
LEFT	Average	1.2403	1.2137	1.2713	1.3379
	Std. Dev.	0.00	0.00	0.00	0.00
RIGHT	Average	1.2178	1.2245	1.2390	1.3028
	Std. Dev.	0.00	0.00	0.00	0.00

Table 10: Calibration factors calculated from the x-ray measurements for the Victoreen® 451P SN: 3796. The additional underlined digits for the calibration factors are kept to avoid rounding errors when the values are used in the calculations, they do not represent the accuracy of the measured calibration factors.

451P, SN 3796		NS80 (2 m Low) 129.06 mR/h	NS80 (3 m Low) 142.92 mR/h	NS80 (1 m High) 532.80 mR/h	NS80 (2 m High) 517.79 mR/h	WS80 (3 m High) 482.40 mR/h
FRONT	Average	1.2761	1.3248	1.3502	1.3265	1.4189
	Std. Dev.	0.00	0.01	0.02	0.00	0.00
LEFT	Average	1.2361	1.2600	1.3658	1.2633	1.3400
	Std. Dev.	0.01	0.01	0.01	0.01	0.00
RIGHT	Average	1.1886	1.2214	1.2999	1.2273	1.3038
	Std. Dev.	0.01	0.01	0.00	0.01	0.00

Table 11: Calibration factors calculated from the x-ray measurements for the Victoreen® 451P-DE-SI SN: 3500. The additional underlined digits for the calibration factors are kept to avoid rounding errors when the values are used in the calculations, they do not represent the accuracy of the measured calibration factors.

451-DE-SI, SN 3500		NS80 (2 m Low) 1.12 mGy/h	NS80 (3 m Low) 1.25 mGy/h	NS80 (2 m High) 4.54 mGy/h	WS80 (3 m High) 4.25 mGy/h
FRONT	Average	1.2406	1.2848	1.3009	1.2827
	Std. Dev.	0.00	0.00	0.02	0.01
LEFT	Average	1.0324	1.0839	1.1687	1.0999
	Std. Dev.	0.01	0.00	0.02	0.01
RIGHT	Average	1.0407	1.0840	1.1367	1.0762
	Std. Dev.	0.01	0.00	0.01	0.01

Conclusions

In this work we studied the response of two different Victoreen instruments as a function of the exposure rate, the instrument orientation and photon energy. The rate dependence for both instruments is of the order of 8 % over the range of exposure rates tested (0.5 mR/h to 1000 mR/h). A significant difference is observed between the two instruments for the orientation dependence investigation. While the Victoreen® 451P shows no significant dependence with instrument orientation, the Victoreen® 451P-DE-SI shows a significant dependence of up to 20 % between the three different orientations. Finally, the measurements of energy dependence of both instruments reveal that the instruments measure lower exposure rate values compared to the reference values for the low energy x-rays by about 20 %. In comparison, for the ^{60}Co gamma-ray beam, both detectors measure 3 % to 5 % higher than the reference value.

Care should be taken in defining the quantity used to determine the field produced by the reference radiation beams (e.g., exposure rate, air-kerma, ambient dose equivalent rate, personal dose equivalent). Furthermore, when using a radiation detection instrument to determine the value of the reference radiation beams, the instrument measurement units shall be taken into account in order to obtain the correct radiation filed value. It is possible that the reference beam is defined in units of Sv/h while the instrument used to perform the measurements displays in R/h. This can introduce a source of error if the appropriate conversion coefficients are not used to convert from R/h to Sv/h or vice versa. The correction due to the conversion coefficients vary with photon energy. The variations are within approximately 2 % and 5 % for ^{60}Co and ^{137}Cs respectively and between 45.5 % and 52 % for x-ray beams and ^{241}Am [3].

When measuring at close distances from the source (1 m or less), with the instrument in the side orientation (Right or Left), corrections should be made to account for the instrument volume effect for both the Victoreen® 451P and the Victoreen® 451P-DE-SI instruments.

Based on this large variation in the calculated exposure rate values for ^{241}Am it is not possible to compare the instruments measurements with a reference exposure rate value.

The dependences observed for each instrument in this work as well as the significant differences observed between each of the instruments can contribute to the explanation of the difference observed between the measurements conducted at the JRC and SRNL described in the introduction of this work.

References

1. Victoreen® 451P & 451P-DE-SI Ion Chamber Survey Meter Operators Manual, http://www.science.mcmaster.ca/medphys/images/files/courses/3A03/451_Ion_Chamber_Survey_Meter.pdf

2. Calibration of x-ray and gamma-ray measuring instruments, P.J. Lamperti and M. O'Brien. NIST Special Publication 250-58.

3. ISO 4037-3, X and gamma reference radiation for calibrating dosemeters and doserate meters and for determining their response as a function of photon energy — Part 3: Calibration of area and personal dosemeters and the measurement of their response as a function of energy and angle of incidence

4. Calibration of a ^{137}Cs Gamma-Ray Beam Irradiator using Large Size Chambers, R. Minniti and S. M. Seltzer, Applied Radiations and Isotopes, Vol. 65 (4), pp. 401-407, 2007.

5. The physics of radiology, 4th Edition, Publisher Charles C. Thomas. Authors: Harold Elford Johns and John Robert Cunningham.

6. J.H. Hubbell and S.M. Seltzer. Tables of x-ray mass attenuation coefficients and mass energy-absorption coefficients 1 keV to 20 MeV for elements Z = 1 to 92 and 48 additional substances of dosimetric interest. NISTIR 5632. May 2005. (http://www.nist.gov/pml/data/xraycoef/index.cfm)

7. Pelowitz D B, ed., MCNPX User's Manual, Version 2.5.0, Los Alamos National Laboratory report LA-CP-05-0369 (April 2005)

8. White M C 2002 Photoatomic Data Library MCPLIB04: A New Photoatomic Library Based on Data from ENDF/B-VI Release 8, Los Alamos National Laboratory Internal Memorandum X-5: MCW-02–111 and LA-UR-03–1019.

9. Laboratoire National Henri Becquerel (LNHB), Recommended Data, http://www.nucleide.org/DDEP_WG/DDEPdata.htm

10. Nuclear Data Center, Brookhaven National Laboratory, Evaluated Nuclear Structure Data File (ENSDF), http://www.nndc.bnl.gov/

11. D.S. Smith and M.G. Stabin. Exposure Rate Constants and Lead Shielding values for over 1,100 Radionuclides, Health Physics The Radiation Safety Journal, Vol. 102, No. 3, pp. 271–291, March 2012.

12. Rad Pro Calculator http://www.radprocalculator.com/Gamma.aspx

13. S.M. Seltzer, "Air-kerma-rate coefficients for selected photon-emitting radionuclide sources." NISIP 7092A (2004).

www.ingramcontent.com/pod-product-compliance
Lightning Source LLC
Chambersburg PA
CBHW081809280526
45789CB00008B/3064